Authentic Log Homes

Restored Timbers for Today's Homesteads

Ferris Robinson

4880 Lower Valley Road, Atglen, PA 19310 USA

Library of Congress Cataloging-in-Publication Data

Robinson, Ferris.
Authentic log homes : restored timbers for today's homesteads /
by Ferris Robinson.
p. cm.
ISBN 0-7643-2191-9 (hardcover)
1. Log cabins—United States. I. Title.

NA8470.R63 2005
728'.37'0973—dc22

2004026123

Designed by "Sue"
Type set in Staccato222 BT/Souvenir Lt BT

ISBN: 0-7643-2191-9
Printed in China

Published by Schiffer Publishing Ltd.
4880 Lower Valley Road
Atglen, PA 19310
Phone: (610) 593-1777; Fax: (610) 593-2002
E-mail: Info@schifferbooks.com

For the largest selection of fine reference books on this and related subjects, please visit our web site at
www.schifferbooks.com
We are always looking for people to write books on new and related subjects. If you have an idea for a book please contact us at the above address.

This book may be purchased from the publisher.
Include $3.95 for shipping.
Please try your bookstore first.
You may write for a free catalog.

In Europe, Schiffer books are distributed by
Bushwood Books
6 Marksbury Ave.
Kew Gardens
Surrey TW9 4JF England
Phone: 44 (0) 20 8392-8585; Fax: 44 (0) 20 8392-9876
E-mail: info@bushwoodbooks.co.uk
Free postage in the U.K., Europe; air mail at cost.

Dedication

I would like to dedicate this book to my husband, Dan Robinson, who gets me into more things. And to my mother, Mary Ferris Kelly, who gets me out.

Contents

Acknowledgments

There are so many people who had a hand in this book. My husband, Dan Robinson, co-owner of Walden Log Homes, offered my services as a copywriter to Schiffer Publishing. The next thing I know, I am writing a book. Tina Skinner, my editor, probably had more faith in me than she should have, but her confidence in my spearheading this project was what actually began this book.

My mother, Mary Ferris Kelly, drew every single plan in this book. They took priority over her career as a painter and sculptor, and the deadlines I imposed were much more demanding than those from her galleries. She also jumped on board as a photo stylist, last-minute-babysitter, and general gofer. I could never get by without her.

The men that actually built these houses, Ray Griffin, Randy Lovern, Terry Kilgore, and Russell Craig worked much like the pioneers on these masterpieces under Scott Kelley's direction.

Michal Howick spent countless hours proofreading, making copies, and, most importantly, correcting my mistakes. She made working on this book a pleasure.

Alex McMahan, photographer extraordinaire, drove for miles and miles and worked for months taking the most beautiful pictures ever.

And the owners of these wonderful homes were all so generous to let us barge in and rearrange their belongings in the quest for the perfect shot.

Thank you all.

Foreword

"I like old things
That time has tried
And proven good and strong and true.
I like old things.
They have a depth unknown
By anything that is new."
– Author unknown

When I was twenty years old, I went to work for an older friend who was in the business of salvaging original log homes. He carefully disassembled homes originally built in the 1800s and re-erected them as "new" homes for his customers. After my friend built a beautiful log home on 200 acres for himself, he decided to retire from the business. So I went into business for myself, doing exactly the same thing. That was the origin of Walden Log Homes, and that was over twenty years ago.

Since then, I have gained a partner, Dan Robinson, my brother-in-law. Together we have expanded our capabilities considerably. We now not only re-erect existing structures, but also build to any plan by re-notching and re-configuring our antique logs. However, the logs are still the same.

All of the logs we use were hand-hewn over one hundred years ago. They were all hewn with a foot adz, which is a long-handled axe with the blade positioned much like a garden hoe. With this tool, the craftsmen would straddle the felled tree, and cut off the bark and soft sap wood on two sides until the dense heart wood was finally shaped into a large square log. And then they would begin again, massive tree after massive tree, until enough heart wood was hewn to make their home.

There are several advantages these reclaimed timbers have over new logs. One is the fact that these logs moved and creaked and twisted, natural properties of all wood as it settles, over 100 years ago. They have done all the moving they are going to do.

Another advantage these logs have is that they were all actually virgin timbers. Our forefathers chose the biggest, strongest trees for their homesteads, and after the "softness" was hewn from them, the dense slow-growth heartwood was, and is, as hard as a rock and naturally resistant to insects and rot.

Aesthetically, these logs are loaded with character. They are not uniform in shape or size; the hewn marks left in them are authentic, not machine-made. The craftsmanship by our settlers is remarkable. You simply cannot get logs like this anymore, and you cannot duplicate this unique, authentic look.

At Walden, we are committed to carrying on the tradition of these 1800s craftsmen. Our goal is to combine these one-of-a-kind logs with modern amenities to provide homes that can be described as nothing less than striking. We hope you agree.

Scott Kelley
Co-owner and founder,
Walden Log Homes, LLC

Introduction

"A man who works with his hands is a laborer; a man who works with his hands and his brain is a craftsman; but a man who works with his hands and his brain and his heart is an artist."

– Louis Nizer

I have spent the past year in awe of the houses in this book that I have been privileged enough to visit. There are so many differences among them. Some are immense, with great vaulted ceilings, and some are much smaller, with great vaulted ceilings. Some have been erected exactly "as found" with the original off-center front door remaining that way. Some have incorporated futuristic elements with the ancient timbers, much like Jane Jetson marrying Daniel Boone. Some are built on endless pastures, some are built on shimmering lakes, and one is built as a guest cottage right in the back yard. But all of them are absolutely captivating.

My own house is in this book. I waited a very long time for it. When I married my husband, he promised if I lived in his "bachelor pad" for three years, we would look for a house together. Seventeen years later, we finally moved out of the "pad" and into the most beautiful log home I have ever seen. Over a year after moving in, I still find myself gazing at the antique heart pine that gleams on the floors and countertops, and thinking how much life it adds to my home. I run my hands over the hand-hewn logs and feel the slashes in them that were made over a century ago. I daydream about the old pegs and notches still left in some of the logs, and wonder how these things were crafted so perfectly so long ago.

Scott Kelley works with his hands and his brain and his heart when he builds these structures. He has respect, if not awe, for the timbers. And when he cuts into them, he does so only after a great deal of consideration. If he had his way, I think every single one would be re-erected exactly "as found" without a single log touched. He is truly an artist. His vision of how these homes should look enables the finished product to be just right.

I look at how perfectly the barn wood cabinets blend in with the stone fireplace and very old logs, and feel a certain wonder at these reclaimed materials. They have been here much, much longer than I have been. And doubtless they will be here longer still than I will be. They are steadfast. They are timeless.

And there is no doubt in my mind that the owners of every single one of these homes are still struck by the strength and beauty of these ancient timbers. Sometimes I wonder what the craftsmen who hewed the logs by hand so long ago would say to see them moved and rebuilt. And I think they would nod with approval and say, "Now that is a mighty fine house. It looks the way a log home is *supposed* to look."

The Old Homestead

The poplar, beech, and chestnut logs in this house pre-date the Revolutionary War. The owner, Mary Ferris Kelly, had a completely different plan in mind for her mountain retreat, but once she saw the tremendous logs, she refused to cut them. Not that Scott Kelley, her son-in-law, would have allowed her to cut the forty-foot logs with 2-foot faces. The new plan began on a brown paper grocery bag, and ended in a family home that is enjoyed by four generations.

Brad Simmons

The deck overlooks miles and miles of state forest. At night, there is only a single light visible on the ridge beyond the eastern valley.

Paul Kelly

The grandchildren named the lake after their grandfather, "Coon" Kelly. A natural spring, rare on a mountain top, made building the lake easy.

Far Left:
Inside, the living room and dining room flow into one another. A stacked stone fireplace rises into the vaulted ceiling.

Left:
Soft green kitchen cabinets and hard-working heart pine countertops, as well as state-of-the-art appliances, make being in the kitchen a pleasure.

Below left and right:
Scott built this bed for his in-laws out of aged tobacco poles. In the master bath, white beaded board is a lovely contrast to the hand-hewn logs.

Brad Simmons

Upstairs, a distressed white painted bed stands out against weathered barn wood, and unusually-shaped beams support the ceiling.

A crooked rhododendron branch makes a whimsical door knob on this barn wood door.

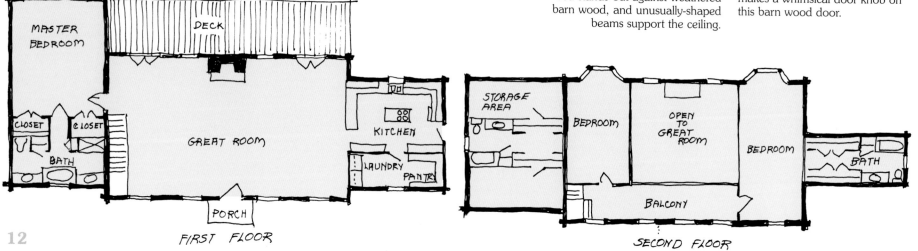

MASTER BEDROOM

DECK

CLOSET   CLOSET

BATH

GREAT ROOM

KITCHEN

LAUNDRY   PANTRY

PORCH

FIRST FLOOR

STORAGE AREA

BEDROOM

OPEN TO GREAT ROOM

BEDROOM

BATH

BALCONY

SECOND FLOOR

High Pasture

Built at the edge of the woods in a seemingly endless meadow, this house feels far away from everything, something Scott Kelley, co-owner and founder of Walden Log Homes, and his wife, Woo, were both intent upon. Without another house in sight, this home-stead appears to have actually been built by pioneers. In fact, axe marks are still evident on these poplar logs, which were hand-hewn over 100 years ago.

Ferris Robinson

Ferris Robinson

In the evenings, Scott and Woo like to ride their horses on the trails that crisscross through their property.

Square-cut heart pine beams were used for support, and rare heart pine poles were used for floor joists. Naturally, both were left exposed.

Ferris Robinson

is Robinson

This hardworking antique table is perfect for rolling out pastry, setting out a buffet or enjoying a cup of Woo's hot spiced tea.

An heirloom quilt, hand stitched by Woo's great-grandmother as a child, is right at home with the log walls, which are at least as old.

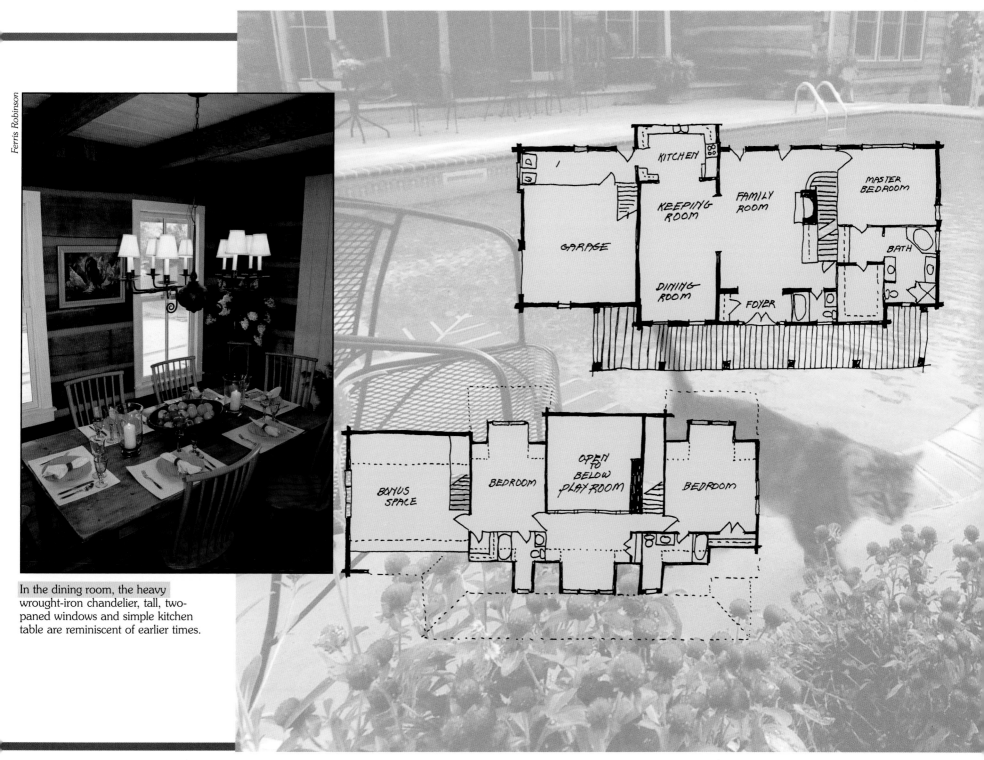

In the dining room, the heavy wrought-iron chandelier, tall, two-paned windows and simple kitchen table are reminiscent of earlier times.

Ferris Robinson

KITCHEN

MASTER BEDROOM

FAMILY ROOM

KEEPING ROOM

GARAGE

BATH

DINING ROOM

FOYER

BONUS SPACE

BEDROOM

OPEN TO BELOW PLAY ROOM

BEDROOM

On Walden Pond

Nestled deep in the woods in Lookout Highlands, this house is a perfect getaway in the north Georgia mountains. On weekends, the owners fish, watch for rare birds, hike to an 80-foot waterfall, and, above all, relax. The timeless hand-hewn logs and pristine setting instantly drain the tensions from a fast-paced life.

19

Alex McMahan

Alex McMahan

After dinner, a short stroll down the path to the pond is usually in order, whether the fish are biting or not. Later, as the crickets and frogs begin their summer symphony, chairs are pulled up to the outdoor fireplace, marshmallows are roasted, and tall tales are told.

It is hard to decide between a nap on the porch swing or a game of checkers on lazy afternoons.

A cathedral ceiling makes the living room seem much larger than it is *(shown on previous page)*, and with the open kitchen, the cook is always in the thick of things. In the breakfast nook, the white painted cupboard echoes the white Kolbe & Kolbe windows.

Opposite page:
The lady of the house is an avid collector of antiques, with a special flair for decorating. She made a headboard out of an antique door, a sink out of a chest she refinished *(shown on page 23)*, and a shelf from an old drawer and a pair of wrought-iron brackets. Off the master bedroom, a sleeping porch is perfect for an early cup of coffee as the sun peeps up through the pines.

The dormitory can sleep at least six little girls, and a nook for the youngest daughter is a favorite reading spot.

The floor plan labels read:

SECOND FLOOR

BEDROOM

OPEN TO BELOW

BEDROOM

dn.

MASTER BEDROOM

SLEEPING PORCH

BREAKFAST

FAMILY ROOM

KITCHEN

PLAY ROOM

UP

COVERED PORCH

Garden in the Woods

This secluded cabin sits amongst mulched paths that wind among oakleaf hydrangeas and day lilies and azaleas. A deep screened-in porch and ample open decking provide lovely choices to enjoy the peaceful grounds.

Alex McMahan

Alex McMahan

Alex McMahan

Alex McMahan

Previous page and above:
The family room is a great gathering spot for this couple's children and grandchildren, while the loft above is a cozy place to play cards or curl up with a good book.

In the kitchen, the ceiling joists are impressive, but the huge round beam, which was salvaged from an old sugar mill, is extraordinary.

Alex McMahan

The rich red hues of the spacious master bedroom set off the ancient logs.

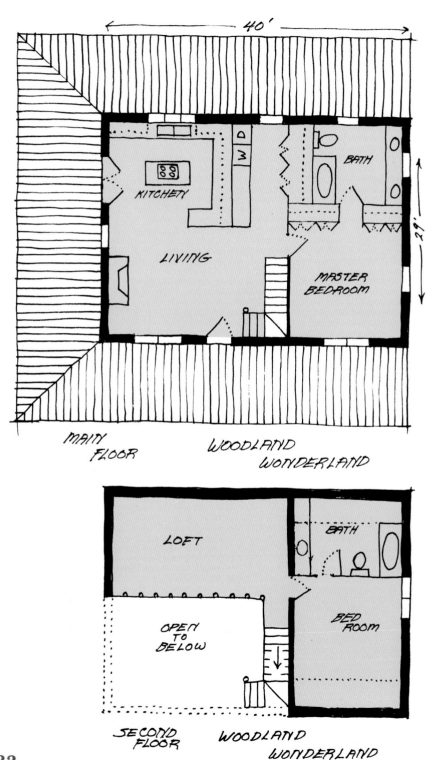

MAIN FLOOR

WOODLAND WONDERLAND

SECOND FLOOR

WOODLAND WONDERLAND

Heart pine was the choice for bathroom vanities, lending warmth and depth to a traditionally cold surface.

Laurel Point

With a blended family of six teenagers, this couple decided a lake getaway was in order. Minutes from their primary home, this cabin is a respite for all. Quiet romantic dinners for the parents are now a possibility, and entertaining both family and friends is a breeze. Both avid fishermen, this couple customarily wets a line after dinner in the large lake a few steps from their back door.

Alex McMahan

Massive hand-hewn beams, a mountain stone fireplace, and antique heart pine flooring anchor this living room, while two-story views of the lake let it soar.

At the heart of the house is an island topped with antique heart pine countertops. Multifaceted, it serves as buffet, lunch counter, and a perfect spot for icing sugar cookies.

Support posts with ancient mortises blend with decorative hand-hewn beams on the ceiling, and rhododendron branches pair with old tobacco poles for a unique staircase. *(Shown here and following two photographs)*.

The dilemma in the master bedroom is whether to enjoy the view of the lake from the sleeping porch deck, or to simply curl up and nap in the afternoon sunlight.

Weathered barn wood and hand-hewn logs soften the bathroom tile.

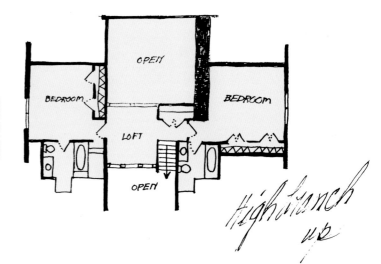

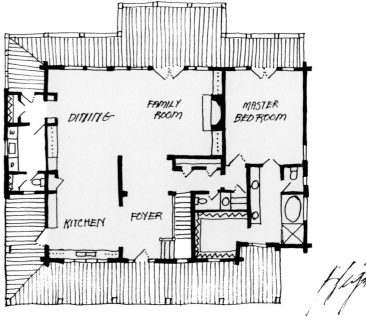

Alex McMahan

Upstairs, both the girls' and boys' dormitories have a full bath and can easily sleep seven each. The closet doors are made of weathered barn wood and maintain the rustic feel of the house.

Dogtrot Revisited

Hidden deep in a thicket of mountain laurel above a rushing stream, this log home is a series of dog trots. Basically two one-room cabins joined by a porch or "dog trot," this style of home was very common a century ago. Vaulted ceilings, skylights, and other modern amenities bring this authentic replica into the twenty-first century.

Alex McMahan

Alex McMahan

42

Avid outdoor enthusiasts, this couple decorated their home with evidence of their passions: snow shoes, sail boats, and a full-sized canoe. Despite the spacious living room, they could not fit in the airplane.

The front door was salvaged from a once beautiful, historic home awaiting the wrecking ball. The bark was intentionally left on the rustic wood trim, and is mirrored exactly on the interior.

Alex McMahan

Details, such as corner work on the logs, exposed brick, hand-hewn timbers, and heart pine flooring, make every inch of this house interesting.

Alex McMahan

In the master bedroom, reclaimed heart pine flooring and chunky wooden furniture make this area calm and relaxing.

45

46

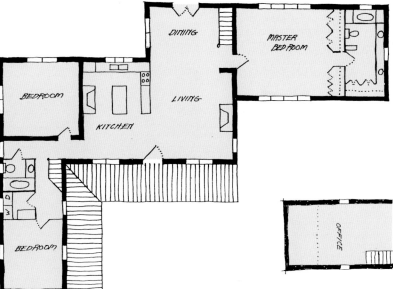

BEDROOM

KITCHEN

DINING

LIVING

MASTER BEDROOM

W D

BEDROOM

OFFICE

The sound of the gurgling creek
and the scent of the laurel in
full bloom make the porch
swing a true paradise.

Rustic Retreat

Built as a getaway for a busy Atlanta couple, this log cabin was re-erected exactly "as-found". Notice the off-center door, and window above. Tall and narrow, the re-erected house more than triples its original living space, yet because the footprint was not altered, not a bit of its pioneer appeal was sacrificed.

After dinner, the children customarily fish for bass in the stocked lake, while the grownups linger around a roaring fire in the outdoor fireplace.

Alex McMahan

Alex McMahan

The newel post, banister, and stair rail were all part of the original house, as were the summer beam and floor joists.

Beautiful antique pieces, as well as more whimsical ones, are a fine fit in this restored log cabin.

Historical purists regarding this cabin, this couple was determined to maintain the integrity of the original craftsmanship. There is not an ounce of sheetrock in the entire structure; weathered barn wood covers the walls.

In the bathrooms, the owner creatively used deer antlers to hold hand towels and toilet paper.

The flooring from the original structure was used in most of the house, but antique heart pine covers the main floor.

An old farmhouse sink, heart pine countertops, and barn wood cabinets make the modern kitchen and breakfast room look as though pioneers actually live here.

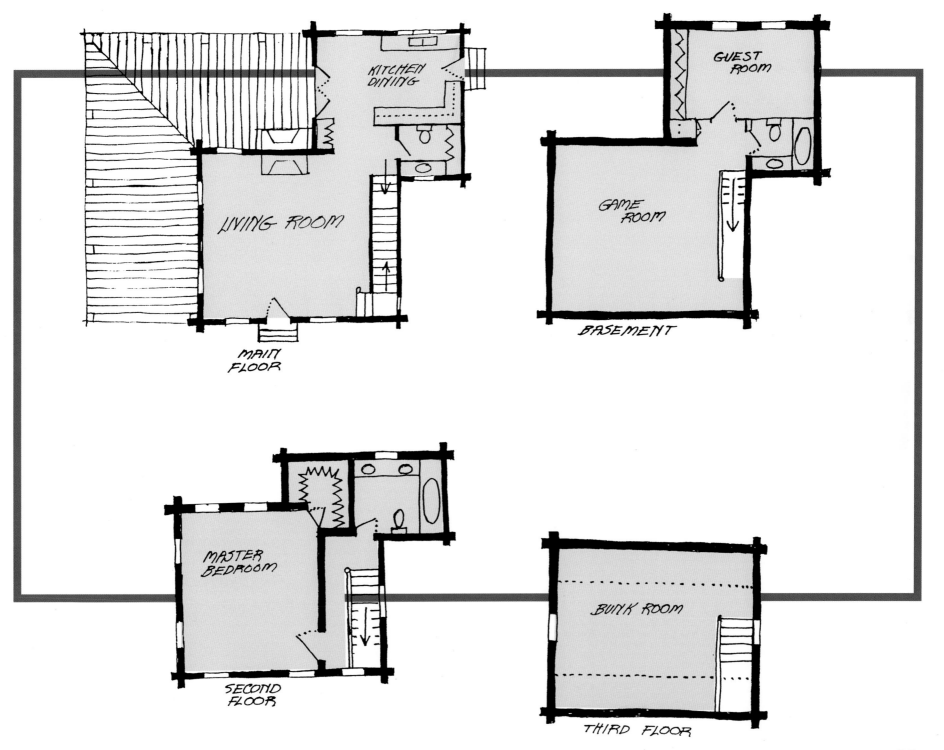

KITCHEN DINING

LIVING ROOM

MAIN FLOOR

GUEST ROOM

GAME ROOM

BASEMENT

MASTER BEDROOM

SECOND FLOOR

BUNK ROOM

THIRD FLOOR

55

Cabin at Twilight

This little cabin is tucked deep in the woods overlooking a vast lake. A deep back porch has rocking chairs on the ready for relaxing as the sun sets over the water.

Ferris Robinson

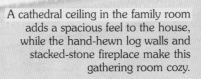

A cathedral ceiling in the family room adds a spacious feel to the house, while the hand-hewn log walls and stacked-stone fireplace make this gathering room cozy.

The kitchen opens to the dining room
and the open shelving displays dishes
as well as collectibles.

An antique sugar chest makes a statement in the front hall, while a six-point buck keeps watch over the house.

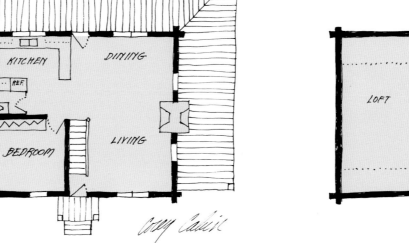

KITCHEN

REF.

DINING

BEDROOM

LIVING

LOFT

cozy Cabin

CORE.
CF.

59

Elder Mountain Lodge

This remarkable house was a collaboration between Scott Kelley and his longtime friend Dwight Parker. Different species of wood, including poplar, oak, pine, chestnut, and cherry were used throughout the house. The support post is actually an uprooted tree, and the siding in the office is from a cherry tree Dwight climbed as a child. When it died during the construction of the house, Dwight planed it down to use instead of sheet rock.

Alex McMahan

Alex McMahan

The open kitchen with its large granite-topped island is a gourmet's dream. A wide hallway leading to the master bedroom turned out to be a perfect nook for a library.

A picture window in the master bedroom makes the owner feel like she is sleeping in the treetops.

The use of natural materials, from stone to a wide range of woods, truly make this house one-of-a-kind.

The rich, finished look of the flooring in the foyer belies the fact that it was originally weathered barn wood.

Alex McMahan

Alex McMahan

Generous porches look out over the top of the forest, giving one the sense of playing in a tree house.

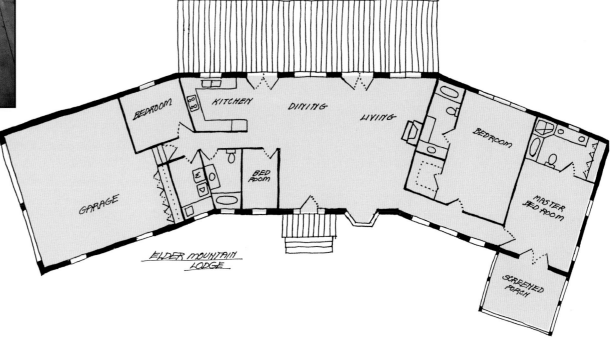

ELDER MOUNTAIN LODGE

Lakeside Cottage

This charming cabin is tucked deep in the woods, and overlooks a lake that beckons to this couple and their children. A respite for their busy lives, this spot is a welcome weekend retreat.

Alex McMahan

The back deck is the perfect spot for gazing through the woods at the water, sipping fresh-squeezed lemonade or, of course, relaxing in the hot tub.

67

Antique heart pine was used abundantly in this house, giving a certain richness to the flooring, stair rails, countertops, and door and window casing.

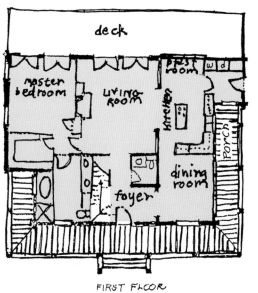

deck

post room | w d

master bedroom

living room

kitchen

porch

dining room

foyer

FIRST FLOOR

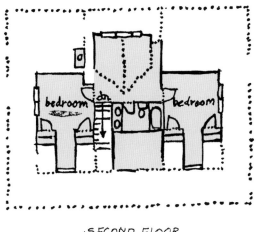

SECOND FLOOR

bedroom | dn | bedroom

69

Hand-hewn beams support the second floor and white linen curtains contrast beautifully with the roughness of the log walls.

High Country

This magnificent home on the western brow was dreamed about for years by its owner. It is the perfect blend of old and new with its hand-hewn logs from the nineteenth century and modern amenities from the twenty-first century.

Brad Simmons

Geometric glass panes rise to the rooftops in the foyer and are mirrored in the rear of the house, opening the home to the great outdoors. In the entry, the heart pine flooring is inlaid with black slate.

The massive stone fireplace fills up the two-story great room. Climbing rope serves as railing on the stairwell and balcony, evidence of the owner's passion for rock climbing. Antique heart pine flooring covers the floors, giving them a distinctive feel.

In the new kitchen, cobalt blue tiles, a commercial-grade stainless steel range and downdraft, and stylish pendant lights contrast with the ancient hand-hewn posts and beams and heart pine floor joists.

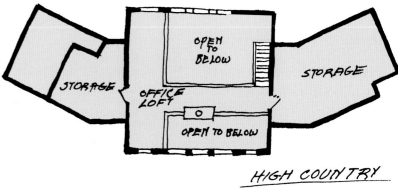

HIGH COUNTRY
SECOND FLOOR

A wealth of wood makes this master bathroom warm and inviting.

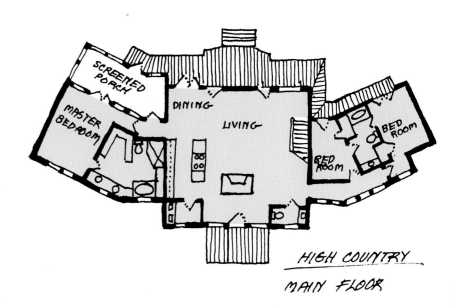

HIGH COUNTRY
MAIN FLOOR

Dot-Dot's Cabin

This little cabin was the lifelong dream of its owner, Dot Henderson. On a shoestring budget, she made every inch of the house pull its weight, and more. Dot loved this place, and lived there happily for two years, before dying suddenly. We like to think she will spend eternity in this place she loved, just not at the same address.

Ferris Robinson

The vaulted ceiling in the family room makes this cozy little cabin live much larger than it is.

An avid collector of antiques, Dot incorporated her lifetime collection of salvaged building materials into her cabin. The front door and diamond-paned side lights, as well as the kitchen island and its columns, had been in Dot's safekeeping for years.

77

Dot did not put doors on the master bedroom, probably so she could hear every rustle her grandchildren made as they slept in the loft above her when they visited.

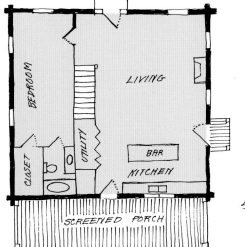

BEDROOM

CLOSET

UTILITY

LIVING

BAR

KITCHEN

SCREENED PORCH

Dot's Cabin
main

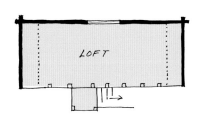

LOFT

Dot's Cabin
loft

Artistic Abode

Six years in the planning, this house was carefully thought out by its owner, Nina Smith. From the curved staircase to the elaborate truss system, every inch of this house was lovingly orchestrated by Nina.

Alex McMahan

A contractor by trade but an artist at heart, Nina found an outlet for her talent while building this house. She etched out, then stained the design on the floor *(shown on the previous page),* as well as stenciled the cabinets in the kitchen. The cat's door was both her idea and design.

Throughout the house, weathered barn wood and hand-hewn beams mingle with forged iron and antique brass.

Alex McMahan

A cathedral ceiling soars over the great room and dining room.

Painted boards accentuate the sloped ceiling in the upstairs bedrooms, and her daughter's armoire was hand-painted by Nina.

Square-cut timbers tie the tiled bathroom to the rest of the house.

85

The boughs of a maple tree cover the back deck, while a tin roof covers the front porch.

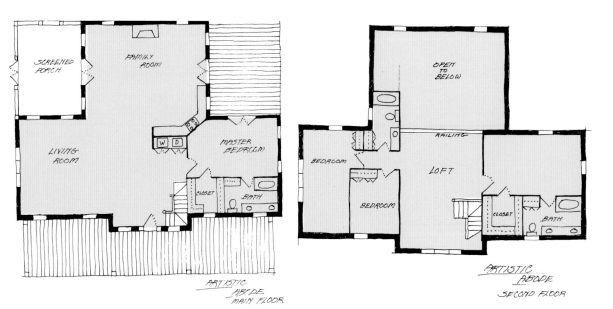

SCREENED PORCH

FAMILY ROOM

LIVING ROOM

W D

MASTER BEDROOM

CLOSET

BATH

ARTISTIC ABIDE
MAIN FLOOR

OPEN TO BELOW

RAILING

BEDROOM

LOFT

BEDROOM

CLOSET

BATH

ARTISTIC ABODE
SECOND FLOOR

Brow Lake

This spacious house features an open floor plan and lots and lots of Kolbe windows and doors. A balcony overlooks the foyer, which is open to all the public rooms of the house. Built on a bluff over-looking the western brow, the deck rails are made of reclaimed 2 x 4s, which are in keeping with the rustic feel of the house.

Alex McMahan

A mortise in this hand-hewn beam was crafted over 100 years ago.

91

A hand-hewn cypress post adds simple delineation in the dining room, while large oak posts separate the kitchen. Antique heart pine was used for flooring as well as kitchen countertops. On the living room side of the island, aged barn wood was used to blend with the cabinetry around the fireplace. Upstairs, the library is lined with barn wood bookcases, which are backed with deep red beaded board.

In the master bed and bath, wide boards were painted creamy white and used instead of sheetrock on the walls and ceiling. The door to the powder room shows the original red paint on the inside, and gray weathered barn wood on the outside.

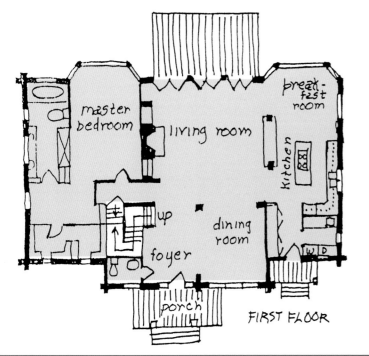

FIRST FLOOR

- master bedroom
- living room
- breakfast room
- kitchen
- up
- dining room
- foyer
- porch
- W/D

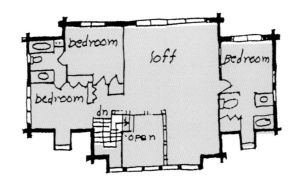

SECOND FLOOR

- bedroom
- loft
- bedroom
- bedroom
- dn
- open

A Guest Cottage

Ferris Robinson

This cabin is actually a guest house that sits on a knoll behind the owner's main house. The Stonington flag, which has sixteen stars and sixteen stripes and is known as the "unofficial" flag of Tennessee, waves proudly in the breeze. It was procured after searching high and low for years, in Mystic River, Pennsylvania, during a family reunion.

Exposed floor joists were painted soft pumpkin to echo the window trim, and authentic wrought iron hardware is used on barn wood doors throughout the house.

Weathered barn wood was used abundantly in this house as siding, ceiling decking, doors, and even as a clever disguise for the meter box. Soft pumpkin doors are a lovely compliment to the rough gray wood.

Ferris Robinson

A hand-hewn beam serves as a high mantle piece over the stacked stone fireplace.

Ferris Robinson

97

Antique heart pine floor joists, creamy white ceiling decking, and weathered barn wood walls add intrigue to the master bedroom. Upstairs, a salvaged Leo #1 stove and antique quilts add interest to the sleeping loft.

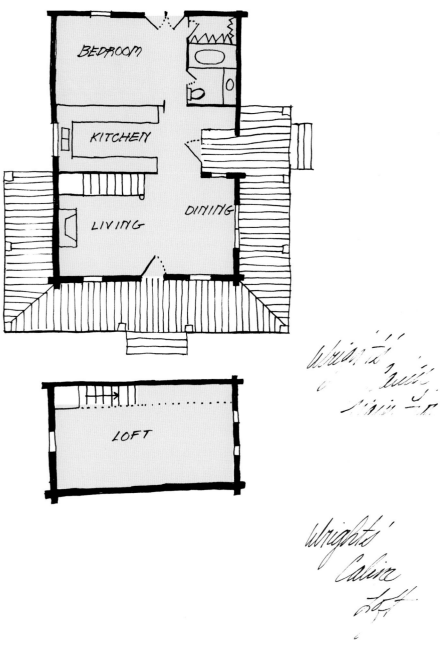

BEDROOM

KITCHEN

LIVING

DINING

LOFT

Wrights'
Cabin
Loft

Avid sailors, this couple used a pulley from a sailboat in the eave of the house.

A River House

Perched on the bank of the Tennessee River, this cabin is enveloped by the blooms of hydrangeas in early summer. The plan for the house was drawn hastily by the owner on a piece of graph paper, yet features a master wing, a vaulted living room, and magnificent views of the river all around. No architect could have designed a more perfect house.

Ferris Robinson

The master bedroom and bath are separated from the two guest bedrooms by the spacious living area.

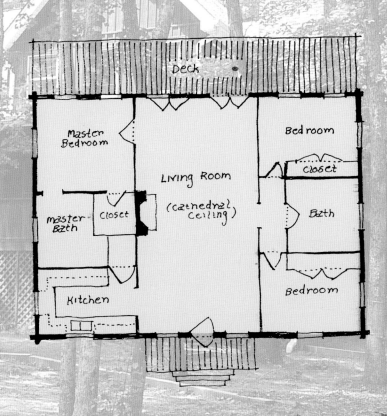

Deck

Master Bedroom

Bedroom

Living Room

Closet

(cathedral ceiling)

Master Bath

Closet

Bath

Kitchen

Bedroom

A screened porch and open deck are a good place to be mesmerized by the ever-changing river — a large bass jumps, a heron flies, and the water laps on the river bank.

Eagle Rock

This log cabin sits on the edge of a bluff and has a wide open view of the valley below. It is a welcome retreat for the owners and their grown children, as well as a multitude of family and friends. With every inch perfectly decorated, this house is truly a pleasure.

In the family room and adjoining dining room, Kolbe & Kolbe French doors lead to the covered porch. In the kitchen, black stained cabinets complement the antique heart pine countertops. Warm to the elbows, heart pine is a friendly surface that is also low maintenance.

Alex McMahan

Alex McMahan

Aged tobacco poles were used for handrails on the staircase. Throughout the house, the rich hue of antique heart pine makes the floors seem to have a life of their own.

Alex McMahan

In the master bedroom, the large striking bed is almost as captivating as the breathtaking view.

Alex McMahan

Alex McMahan

The simple white cabinets in the master bath play up the roughness of the reclaimed logs. Upstairs, soft green beaded board paneling and a sloped ceiling make the charming bathroom irresistible.

Upstairs, weathered barn wood takes
the place of sheetrock, and decorative hand-hewn beams tie the
bedrooms in with the rest of the
house.

Watching the sun set over the western valley is an easy way to spend a summer evening.

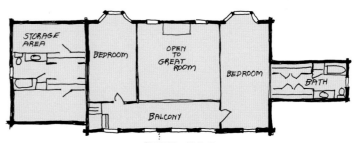

STORAGE AREA

BEDROOM

OPEN TO GREAT ROOM

BEDROOM

BATH

BALCONY

SECOND FLOOR

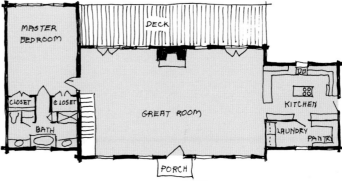

MASTER BEDROOM

DECK

CLOSET

CLOSET

GREAT ROOM

KITCHEN

BATH

LAUNDRY

PANTRY

PORCH

FIRST FLOOR

113

Log Cabin Antiques and Herbs

Ferris Robinson

A formal herb garden thrives on the sunny side of this lovely old cabin. Inside, a breathtaking collection of period antiques are for sale by the proprietress, who is well into her eighties.

A roaring fire, hot spiced tea, and homemade lemon pound cake makes stopping by the shop in winter a cozy tradition, while simply gazing at the spectacular herbs make a summer-time visit rewarding.

Ferris Robinson

Hydrangeas, bitter sweet, and lavender are just a few of the flowers that are dried from the exposed rafters at summer's end. During their blooming season, they are used for a wide variety of aromatic lotions, oils, and balms, all hand-made by the owner, Mary Rankin.

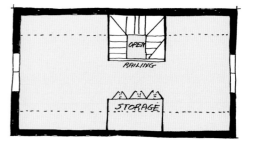

LOG CABIN
ANTIQUES
SECOND FLOOR

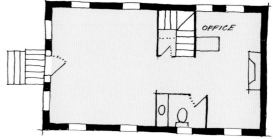

LOG CABIN
ANTIQUES
MAIN FLOOR

Lone Star Lodge

Native Texans, this couple's heritage is evident in their antique log home. A saddle, cowboy boots, and a lasso are reminiscent of the owner's rodeo days as a bull rider, which his childhood sweetheart ingeniously displays.

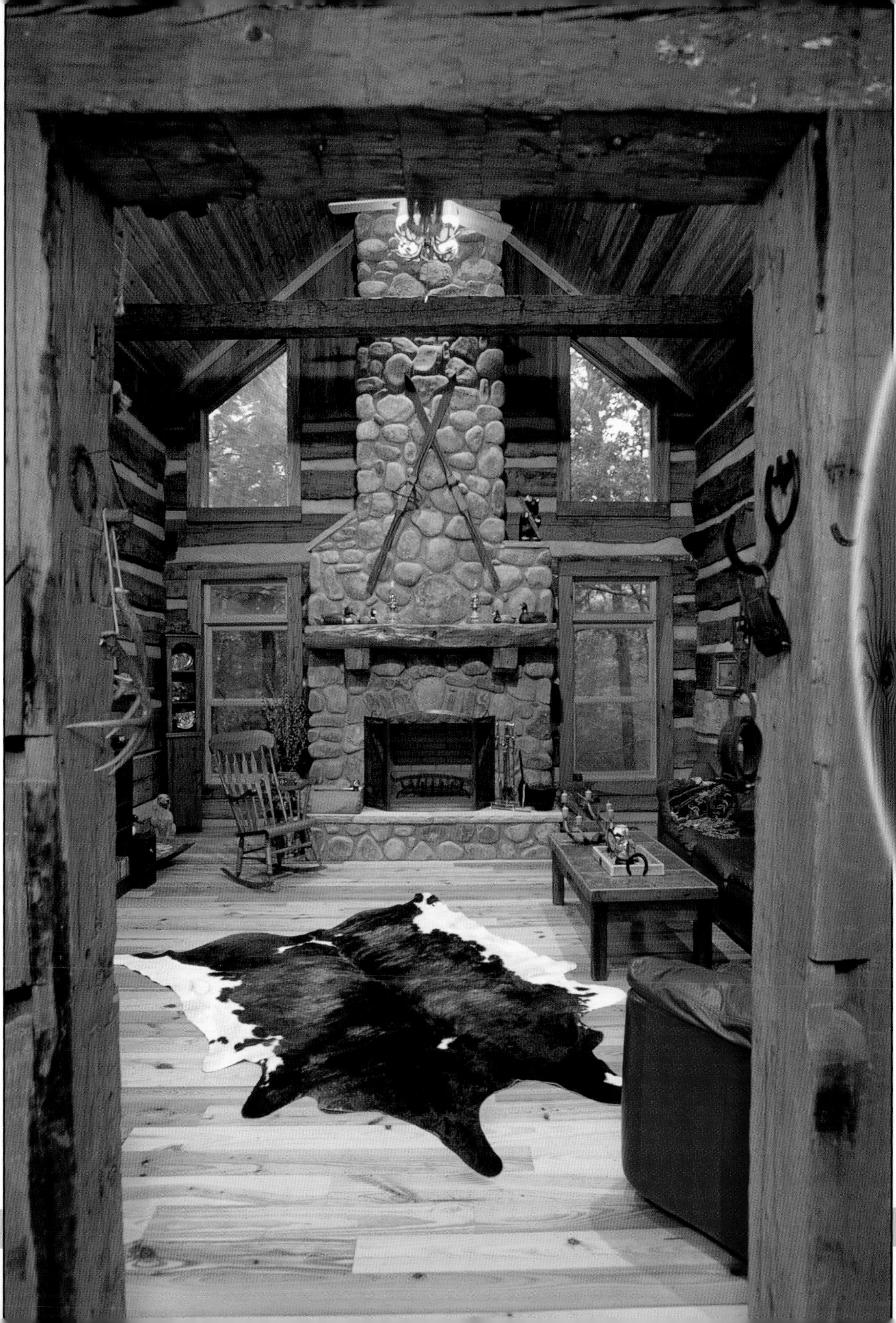
Alex McMahan

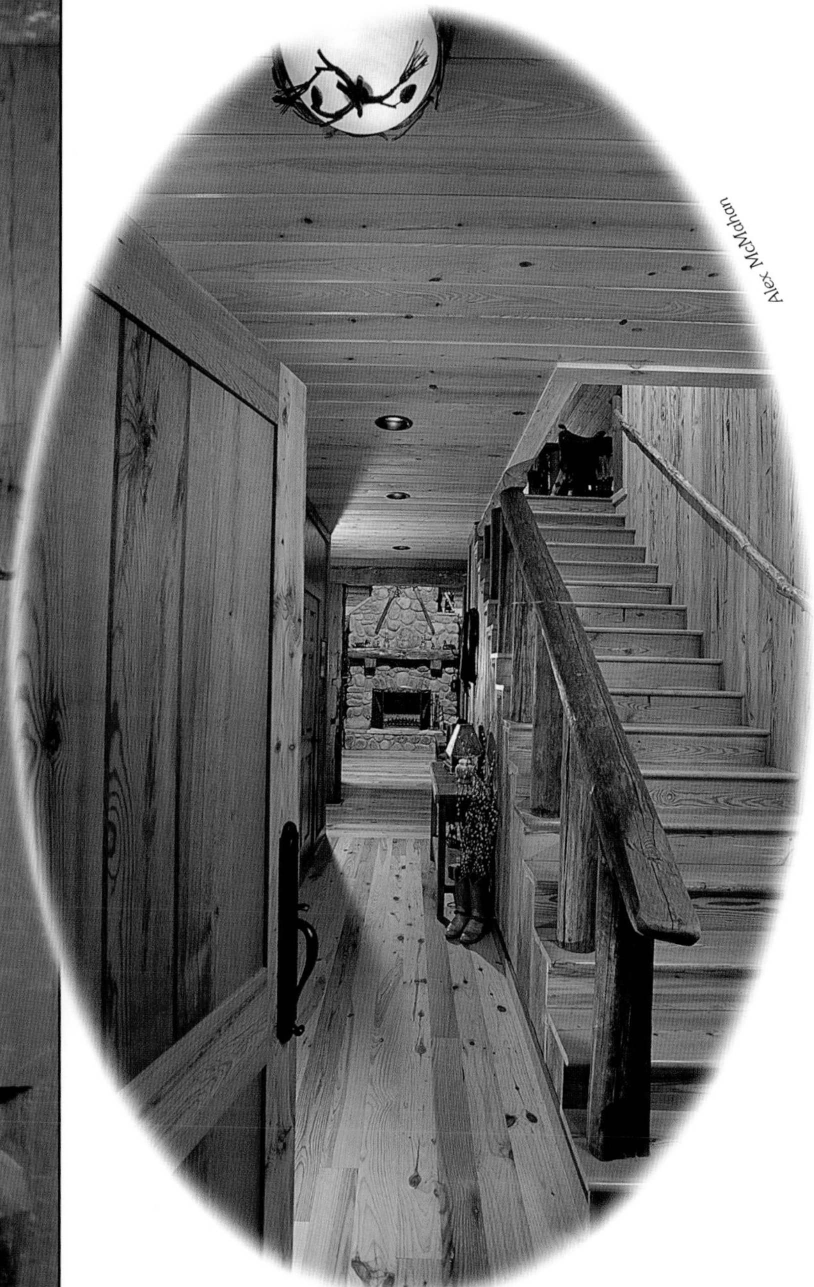
Alex McMahan

The materials in this house, river rock, reclaimed logs, and antique heart pine, make it seem this brand new house has been here forever.

The deep red glazed walls in the foyer accentuate the well-worn simplicity of the logs and barn wood. Its rich color is echoed throughout the house.

Left:
A hand-hewn post serves as a support post in the dining room, and another one displays a collection of cast iron skillets in the kitchen.

In the master suite, French doors open to a deck, and a claw-footed tub lets the bather gaze into the woods.

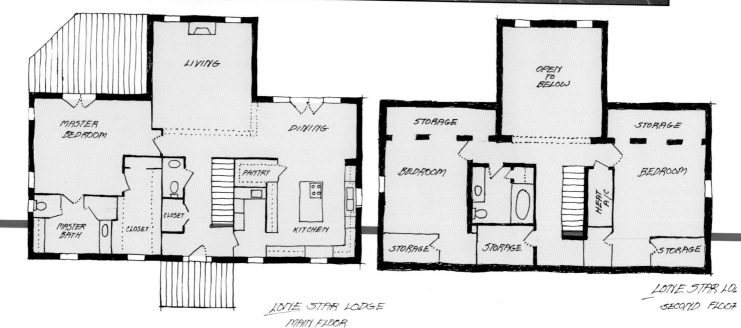

LONE STAR LODGE
MAIN FLOOR

LONE STAR LO.
SECOND FLOOR

Old Lone Cone

A perennial garden thrives along a split rail fence, and various barns serve as picturesque storage areas. A front porch with shaggy cedar posts is an inviting spot to watch the wide range of birds that seem to call this lovely spot home.

Ferris Robinson

Carved from a single gigantic tree trunk over one hundred years ago, this trough has been used as a soaking pool, an ice chest for parties, and a perfect hiding spot for "hide & seek" in the past decade. Before that, its purpose is anyone's guess.

Ferris Robinson

Bottom left:
Several log structures, left by the previous owner, make charming storage buildings.

Left:
The kitchen cabinetry was all made by Tommy Hobbs, a lifelong friend of Scott Kelley's, and an excellent craftsman.

Antique heart pine is used for exposed floor joists, kitchen countertops, and door and window trim, adding to this home's seamless flow.

131

French doors off the master bedroom lead to a covered porch. Log work throughout the house lends a depth to brand new materials.

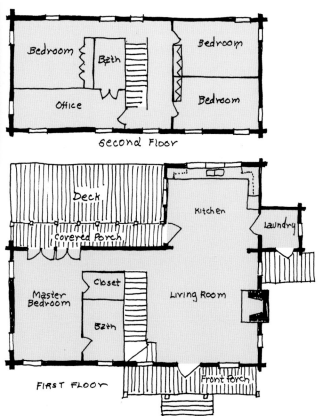

Second Floor

Bedroom

Bath

Office

Bedroom

Bedroom

First Floor

Deck

Kitchen

Laundry

Covered Porch

Closet

Master Bedroom

Living Room

Bath

Front Porch

Briar Branch

This gracious cabin has a welcoming front porch as well as a relaxing back porch by the swimming pool. Inside, the heart pine floor joists support the high ceiling and heart pine flooring gives a timeless feel to the family room. The creamy white kitchen cabinets provide contrast, while the tobacco poles blend in seamlessly.

Alex McMahan

The axe marks on these logs were made by hand over 100 years ago. Nails imbedded sometime at the turn of the nineteenth century were not disturbed.

In the master bedroom, antique pieces are mixed with twig furniture, and new wood on the ceiling blends with hand-hewn support beams and reclaimed heart pine flooring. Natural stone in the master bath was carefully chosen to compliment the logs.

In the den upstairs, a television set seems to be out of place with the antique spinning wheel, hand-hewn logs, and worn tobacco poles.

MASTER BED ROOM

LIVING ROOM

KITCHEN

BRIAR BRANCH
down

BED ROOM

BEDROOM

STORAGE

BRIAR BRANCH

Alex McMahan

Low Valley Farm

Sited where the forest meets the meadow, this spacious house has weathered barn wood in the eaves, a mountain stone fireplace on the front of the house, and a deep front porch that says, "Welcome Home!".

Tobacco poles, barn wood, and heart pine were used extensively throughout the house, making it seem like the house has been here forever.

In the open kitchen, a tree, its bark long worn away, supports the second floor.

Barn wood cabinets with heavy black hardware contrast with white tile and white woodwork in the master bath. Heavy pieces of furniture were used in the bedrooms; smaller pieces would have seemed lost.

Alex McMahan

LOFT

BEDROOM

OPEN TO
GREAT ROOM

ATTIC

SECOND FLOOR

SUN ROOM

KITCHEN

W D

BEDROOM

GREAT ROOM

BEDROOM

PORCH

FIRST FLOOR

Upstairs, a reading loft and a child's bedroom share decorative hand-hewn beams and barn wood siding.

Boston Branch

With nine children and a slew of grandchildren, this family needed a retreat for family get-togethers. The vast grounds provide ample space for family volleyball games, ping pong on the porch, storytelling around the fire, and just resting under the giant oaks as the sun sets over the lake.

Alex McMahan

Alex McMahan

The vaulted great room has two sitting rooms under the massive hand-hewn support beam. The first house Scott Kelley built through Walden Log Homes, this house is "as solid as a rock, and a true work of art" according to the owner.

In the foyer, a combination of hand-painted Italian tile, large geometric panes of glass, and ancient hand-hewn timbers make quite a statement.

Scott had the iron trusses made for the support beams at a local foundry.

150

More often than not, the generous bedrooms host a multitude of grandchildren and their friends.

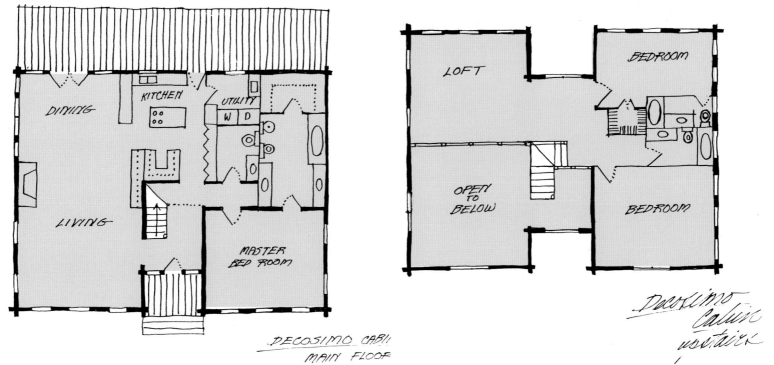

DECOSIMO CABIN
MAIN FLOOR

A Family Farm

This house sits on a vast acreage of farmland overlooking a bluff. Built as a getaway for a couple and their young children, this home is rarely empty. Friends and family gravitate to this lovely spot for horseback riding, fishing, and just plain relaxing.

Porches wrap around the house and feature rough cedar posts and railing, as well as an outdoor mountain stone fireplace.

LAUNDRY 15¢

Left:
Heart pine floor joists rest on enormous support beams, and weathered barn wood is used as ceiling decking as well as for hand-crafted interior doors.

Below & right:
Upstairs, barn wood covers the vaulted ceiling in the den, and is also used for window trim. Large Kolbe windows let in the beautiful views. Bunk beds were crafted from cedar wood by Chattanoogan Cartter Frierson and are as sturdy as they look.

Alex McMahan

Alex McMahan

157

A large hand-hewn log was used as a vanity top in a bathroom, adding infinite interest to hand washing.

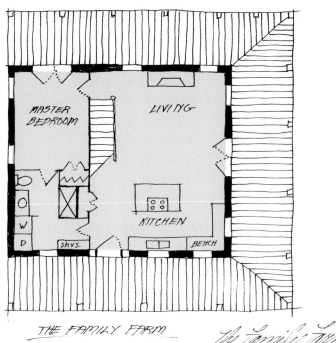

THE FAMILY FARM

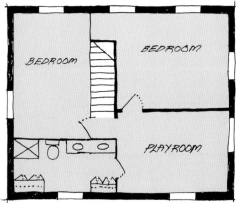

THE FAMILY FARM
SECOND FLOOR

158

Mountain Top Lodge

This welcoming house is decorated with fabrics from Europe and antiques that have been both inherited and collected. The roughness of the massive hand-hewn posts and beams offset the delicate nature of their surroundings.

Alex McMahan

The bank of windows in the kitchen look over the tree tops, while French doors lead to the deck.

Alex McMahan

Thought was given to every nook and cranny of this house; as much attention was given to the ceilings as was to the bedspreads and window treatments.

Antiques are used creatively in the powder room and loft.

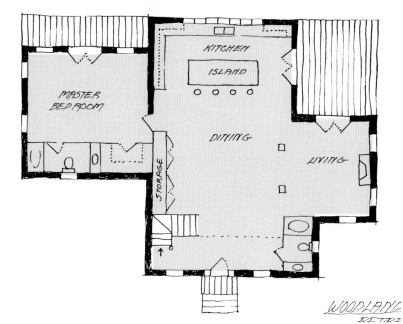

KITCHEN

ISLAND

MASTER
BEDROOM

STORAGE

DINING

LIVING

WOODLAND
RETREAT

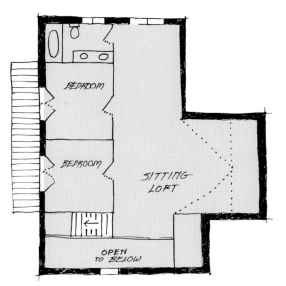

BEDROOM

BEDROOM

SITTING
LOFT

OPEN
TO BELOW

WOODLAND
RETREAT

SECOND FLOOR

Red River Ranch

The scenery surrounding this house is awe-inspiring, but the massive reclaimed timbers used to build the home can hold their own. Set against a forest of spruce, pine, and aspen, this house looks out on a view of Wheeler Peak, the highest point in New Mexico.

Ed Scott

Inside, gilded mirrors and exquisite fabrics mix beautifully with reclaimed timbers, timeworn barn wood, and a very old mantle.

Creamy white cabinets and woodwork *(shown on the previous page)*, as well as rich red fabrics, help show off the venerable logs.

Ed Scott

The use of weathered barn wood, hand-hewn timbers, and a collection of chandeliers lend both consistency and charm throughout the house.

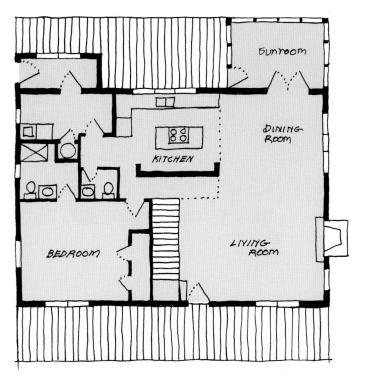

SUNROOM

DINING ROOM

KITCHEN

BEDROOM

LIVING ROOM

RED RIVER RANC,
MAIN FLOOR

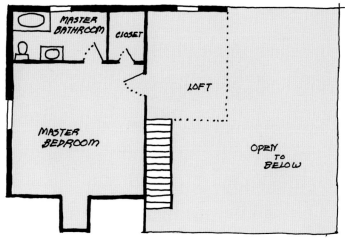

MASTER BATHROOM

CLOSET

LOFT

MASTER BEDROOM

OPEN TO BELOW

RED RIVER RANCH
SECOND FLOOR

171

Wildflower Farm

Marty Jones

This breathtaking setting near Vail, Colorado, couldn't be a better spot for a Walden log home. Built as a nursery, the metal roof is actually new, but is designed to show age immediately.

Inside, the worn log faces display all sorts of gifts and collectibles. Mighty timbers are a quiet, powerful background against a myriad of merchandise.

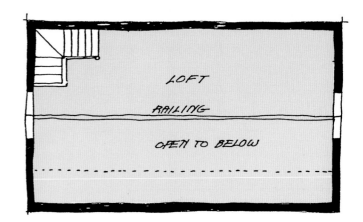

WILDFLOWER FARM

SECOND FLOOR

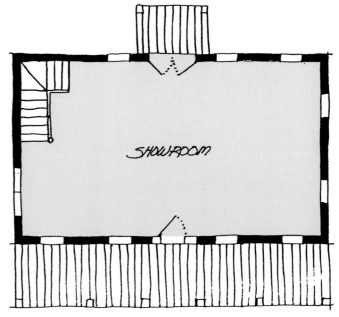

WILDFLOWER FARM NURSERY

MAIN FLOOR

The rocking chair on the porch is actually for sale, but the hand-hewn logs are here to stay.

Resources

Walden Log Homes, LLC
P.O. Box 366
Lookout Mountain, TN 37350
(423)821-8070
(888)332-5647
www.waldenloghomes.com
info@waldenloghomes.com
   Antique log homes, hand-hewn beams, weathered barn wood,
antique heart pine flooring, Kolbe windows and doors

Alex McMahan Photography
P.O. Box 29
Chattanooga, TN 37401
(423)504-6423
alexmcmahan@comcast.net
   Photography

Kolbe Millwork Co., Inc
1323 South 11th Ave.
Wausau, WI 54401
(800) 955-8177
www.kolbe-kolbe.com
   Windows and doors

Tommy Hobbs Woodworking
1310 Taft Highway
Signal Mountain, TN 37377
423-886-5437
thobbtcb@juno.com
   Cabinetry, woodworking

Rustic Alpine Furniture
4273 Scenic Highway
Rising Fawn, GA 30738
(706)398-1315
TCF@rusticalpinefurniture.com
   Woodworking

Cessna Decosimo
1427 Williams St.
Chattanooga, TN 37408
423-266-0733
   Sculpting, painting